Weekly Reader Books presents

THE GIGANTIC JOKE BOOK

BY
JOSEPH ROSENBLOOM
ILLUSTRATIONS BY JOYCE BEHR

STERLING PUBLISHING CO., INC. NEW YORK

Also by Joseph Rosenbloom

Bananas Don't Grow on Trees
Biggest Riddle Book in the World
Daffy Dictionary
Doctor Knock-Knock's Official Knock-Knock
    Dictionary
Funny Insults & Snappy Put-Downs
How Do You Make an Elephant Laugh?
The Looniest Limerick Book
    in the World
Mad Scientist
Monster Madness
Polar Bears Like It Hot
Ridiculous Nicholas Pet Riddles
Ridiculous Nicholas Riddle Book
Silly Verse (and Even Worse)

This book is a presentation of
Weekly Reader Books

Weekly Reader Books offers
book clubs for children from
preschool through junior high school.
All quality hardcover books are selected by
a distinguished Weekly Reader Selection Board.

For further information write to:
Weekly Reader Books
1250 Fairwood Ave.
Columbus, Ohio 43216

With love to Michelle Halfon

Seventh Printing, 1982
Copyright © 1978 by Joseph Rosenbloom
Published by Sterling Publishing Co., Inc.
Two Park Avenue, New York, N.Y. 10016
Distributed in Australia by Oak Tree Press Co., Ltd.
P.O. Box K514 Haymarket, Sydney 2000, N.S.W.
Distributed in the United Kingdom by Blandford Press
Link House, West Street, Poole, Dorset BH15 1LL, England
Distributed in Canada by Oak Tree Press Ltd.
% Canadian Manda Group, 215 Lakeshore Boulevard East
Toronto, Ontario M5A 3W9
Manufactured in the United States of America
Library of Congress Catalog Card No: 77-93310
Sterling ISBN 0-8069-4590-7 Trade
4591-5 Library
7514-8 Paper

Contents

1 Quickies

Advice to worms: Sleep late!

Did you hear about the cannibal who liked to stop where they serve truck drivers?

Doorman: Your car is at the door, sir.
Car Owner: Yes, I hear it knocking.

Flip: Do you live in a small house?
Flop: Small! Ours is the only house in town with round-shouldered mice.

Patient: Doctor, will you treat me?
Doctor: Absolutely not! You'll have to pay the same as everyone else.

Silly: What did the police do when 200 hares escaped from the rabbit farm?
Sillier: They combed the area.

There is a new book out called *How to Be Happy without Money*. It costs ten dollars.

Sign on a cleaning store specializing in gloves:
WE CLEAN YOUR DIRTY KIDS

Customer (at nut counter): Who's in charge of the nuts around here?
Clerk: One moment, please, and I'll take care of you.

Did you hear about the banker who could no longer ride a bike because he lost his balance?

Customer: What dishes do you have for me to eat?
Waiter (in a horrified voice): You eat dishes?

Sign on used car lot:
SECOND-HAND CARS IN FIRST-CRASH CONDITION.

One skeleton to the other: "If we had any guts, we'd get out of here."

Father to son: I don't care if the basement wall *is* cracking. Please stop telling everyone you come from a broken home.

Did you hear about the snake charmer who married an undertaker? They now have towels marked "Hiss" and "Hearse."

Flip: If you were in a jungle by yourself and an elephant charged you, what would you do?

Flop: Pay him.

"Hello, operator, I'd like to speak to the king of the jungle."

"I'm very sorry, but the lion is busy."

Tip: Please tell me the story about the girl who bleached her hair.

Top: Absolutely not. I never tell off-color stories.

Tip: Why are you putting iodine on your paycheck?

Top: Because I just got a cut in my salary.

Advertisement:

For sale: Large crystal vase by lady slightly cracked.

My dog likes to eat garlic. Now his bark is *much* worse than his bite.

They laughed when they saw me sit down at the piano with both hands tied behind my back. They didn't know I played by ear.

You'll be revered one day, Paul.

I don't give a fig about you, Newton.

Famous last words of Eli Whitney: "Keep your cotton-pickin' hands off my gin."

Popular monster song: "A pretty ghoul is like a malady . . ."

Mother monster to little son: Please don't set in that chair! We're saving it for Rigor Mortis to set in.

Sign outside a restaurant:
DON'T STAND OUTSIDE AND BE MISER-ABLE—COME INSIDE AND BE FED UP.

My cellar is so damp, when I lay a mousetrap, I catch fish.

Nip: The garbage man is here.
Tuck: Tell him we don't want any.

Sign in a restaurant window:
EAT NOW—PAY WAITER.

Teacher: Spell Tennessee, Johnny.
Johnny: One-a-see, two-a-see . . .

As the man said when he dented his new car, "Oh well, that's the way the Mercedes-Benz."

Porky Pig: I never sausage heat.
Priscilla Pig: Yes, I'm almost bacon.

Hot weather never bothers me. I just throw the thermometer out of the window and watch the temperature drop.

Every time I get on a ferry it makes me cross.

I was teacher's pet.
She couldn't afford a dog.

Laugh and the world laughs with you; cry and your mother takes your temperature.

Did you hear about the two boas who got married? They had a crush on each other.

Did you hear about the couple who met in a revolving door? They're still going around together.

Husband: My hair is getting thinner.
Wife: So what? Who wants fat hair?

He: Do you like my company?
She: I don't know. What company are you with?

Wise man says:
The bigger the summer vacation, the harder the fall.

Old refrigerators never die, they just lose their cool.

Show me a dog in the middle of a muddy road, and I'll show you a mutt in a rut.

Show me a pink polka-dot pony, and I'll show you a horse of a different color.

Show me a thirsty tailor and I'll show you a dry cleaner.

Teacher: Joseph, name two pronouns.
Joseph: Who, me?
Teacher: Correct!

Clara: Do you realize it takes three sheep to make one sweater?
Sarah: I didn't even know they could knit.

My dog is a terrible bloodhound. I cut my hand once and he fainted.

Ernie: Does your dog have a license?
Bernie: No, she's not old enough to drive.

Wise man says:
    When in doubt, mumble.

Nit: Blood is thicker than water.
Wit: So is toothpaste.

The study of language can be ridiculous sometimes. I heard of someone who is beginning Finnish.

He didn't know the meaning of the word "fear." (He was too afraid to ask.)

To waiter: Who made this Caesar salad—Brutus?

Did you hear about the hippie who starved to death rather than have a square meal?

"Waiter, please get that fly out of my soup. I want to dine alone."

Why don't you go to a tailor and have a fit!

There's a scale over there. Go weigh!

Why don't you learn to play the guitar and stop picking on me?

Flap: Hello, old top! New car?
Jack: No, old car. New top.

Taxi Driver: Look outside and see if my blinker is on.
Passenger: Yes-no-yes-no-yes-no.

Sign in car wrecker's lot:
  RUST IN PEACE.

Did you hear about the elephant who went to the beach to see something new in trunks?

Doctor: How did you get here so fast?
Patient: Flu.

Patient: What does the X-ray of my head show?
Doctor: Nothing.

"I told you not to swallow!" yelled the dentist. "That was my last pair of pliers."

Sign in a nursery:
  ALL BABIES ARE SUBJECT TO CHANGE WITHOUT NOTICE.

No matter how you feel about warts, they have a way of growing on you.

Are you a man or a mouse? Squeak up!

He's so weak, when he tries to whip cream, the cream wins.

A 12-foot pole for people who wouldn't touch things with a 10-foot pole—

A new spinning top that is also a whistle. Now you can blow your top—

A new doctor doll. You wind it up and it operates on batteries.

Waiter: These are the best eggs we've had for years.

Customer: Well, bring me some you haven't had around for that long.

Show me a doctor with greasy fingers and I'll show you a medicine dropper.

Doctor: Did you take the patient's temperature?

Nurse: No, is it missing?

City Boy: Is it easy to milk a cow?
Farm Boy: Any jerk can do it.

Dit: My grandfather was a Pole.
Dot: North or South?

Nita: I lived for a week on a can of sardines.
Rita: How did you keep from falling off?

If the world is getting smaller, how come they keep raising the postal rates?

First Cannibal: Am I late for supper?
Second Cannibal: Yes, everyone's already eaten.

Customer: Waiter, bring me some turtle soup and make it snappy!

Customer: Do you have pickled herring?
Waiter: No, but we have stewed tomato.

Waiter (to customer): Don't complain about the coffee. You may be old and weak yourself some day.

I never forget a face, but in your case I'll make an exception.

"Will you pass the nuts, teacher?"
"No. I think I'll flunk them."

2 Tots
Talk Back

Sam had just completed his first day at school.

"What did you learn today?" asked his mother.

"Not enough," said Sammy. "I have to go back tomorrow."

A ten-year-old boy was told to take care of his younger sister while his parents went into town on business. He decided to go fishing and took his little sister along.

"I'll never do that again," the boy complained to his mother that night. "I didn't catch a thing."

Mother said, "I'm sure she will be quiet next time, if you just explain to her that the fish run away when there's noise."

"It wasn't the noise," the boy said. "She ate the bait."

First Kid: Why don't you take the bus home?
Second Kid: No thanks, my mother would only make
me bring it back.

Little Igor: What does your mother do for a headache?
Little Boris: She sends me out to play.

Billy: I got a hundred in school today.
Mother: That's wonderful, Billy. What did you get a
hundred in?
Billy: Two things. I got 50 in spelling and 50 in
arithmetic.

Little Girl: I'd like to buy a puppy, sir. How much do
they cost?
Store Owner: Ten dollars apiece.
Little Girl: How much does a whole one cost?

16

Junior: Pop, I can tell you how to save money.

Father: That's fine. How?

Junior: Remember you promised me $5 if I got passing grades?

Father: Yes.

Junior: Well, you don't have to pay me.

First Kid: Boy, was I in hot water last night!

Second Kid: How come?

First Kid: I took a bath.

An angry mother took her eight-year-old son to the doctor's office and asked: "Is a boy of eight able to perform an appendix operation?"

"Of course not," the doctor replied.

The mother turned to the boy angrily, "I told you so, didn't I? Now put it back!"

"Sam's parents are sending him to camp for the summer."

"Does he need a vacation?"

"No, they do."

A small boy went to school for the first time. When he came home, he was asked what school was like.

"Nothing much happened," explained the little boy, "except that some lady didn't know how to spell cat. I told her."

Mother: Johnny, what is all the racket from the pantry?

Johnny: I'm busy fighting temptation.

Harold was home from college for the holidays. He said to his little sister, Suzie, "Would you like me to read you a narrative?"

"What is a narrative?" Suzie asked.

"A narrative is a tale," Harold told her.

That night when Suzie went to bed, Harold asked, "Should I extinguish the light, Suzie?"

Suzie asked, "What does extinguish mean?"

"Extinguish means to put out," Harold explained.

The next day they were at dinner when their dog made a nuisance of himself.

"Harold," Suzie said, "would you take the dog by the narrative and extinguish him?"

Teacher: Willie, please spell the word "pole."
Willie: P-O-L.
Teacher: But what is at the end of it?
Willie: Electric wires. But I can't spell that yet.

Mother: Did you go to the party?
Daughter: No. The invitation said from three to six, and I'm seven.

"Dad, where were you born?"
"Chicago."
"Where was Mommy born?"
"Dallas."
"And where was I born?"
"Philadelphia."
"Amazing how we three got together, isn't it?"

A Texas lad rushed home from kindergarten class and insisted his mother buy him a set of pencils, holsters and a gun belt.

"Whatever for, dear?" his mother asked. "You're not going to tell me you need them for school?"

"Yes, I do," he replied. "Teacher said that tomorrow she's going to teach us how to draw."

Two young children stood in front of a mummy case in the museum. On the bottom of the mummy case they noticed "1286 B.C."

"What does that number mean?" asked the first one.

The second one thought a moment and said, "That must be the license number of the car that hit him."

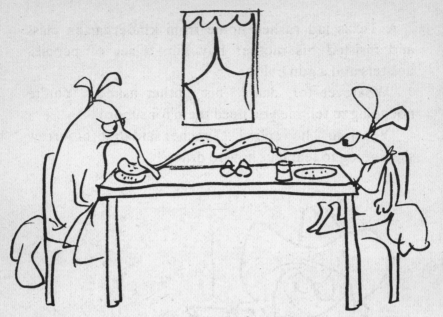

Mother: Harold, stop reaching across the table. Haven't you got a tongue?

Harold: Yes, mother, but my arm is longer.

Junior: When I grow up I want to have a million dollars, a big house, and no bathtubs.

Mother: Why no bathtubs?

Junior: Because I want to be filthy rich.

Doctor: The best time to bathe is just before retiring.

Kid: You mean I don't have to take another bath until I'm almost 65 years old?

A small boy explaining to his father why his report card was so bad, "Naturally I may seem stupid to my teacher, but that's only because she's a college graduate."

Suzie: What time is it?

Father: Three o'clock.

Suzie: Oh no, not again!

Father: What's the matter?

Suzie: I've been asking people for the time all day, and everyone I ask tells me something different.

A prisoner escaped from jail and said to a little boy he met, "Hooray! I'm free! I'm free!"

"So what?" replied the little boy, "I'm four!"

Little Al: Ouch! My new shoes hurt me.

Big Al: No wonder! You have them on the wrong feet.

Little Al: But I don't have any other feet!

Mother: Did you thank Mrs. Smith for the lovely party she gave?

Little Audrey: No, mummy. The girl leaving before me thanked her, and Mrs. Jones said, "Don't mention it," so I didn't.

"Can you read and write?" the woman asked Tommy.

"I can write," Tommy replied, "but I can't read."

"Well, then, let me see how you write your name."

Tommy wrote something on a piece of paper and handed it to the woman.

"What is this?" she asked as she tried to make out the scribbling.

"I don't know," Tommy answered. "I told you I couldn't read."

Junior wrote a letter from camp:
  Dear Mom,
  What's an epidemic?
     Signed, Junior

Suzie: Mom, can I go out and play?
Mom: With those holes in your socks?
Suzie: No, with the kids next door.

I don't like spinach and I'm glad I don't like it, because if I did like it I'd eat it—and I hate the stuff.

A man was putting up a knotty pine wall in the living room. His young son was curious, "What are those holes for?" he asked.

"They're knotholes," replied his father.

"If they're not holes," the boy asked puzzled, "then what are they?"

Father: Well, son, how are your marks?
Son: Under water.
Father: What do you mean?
Son: Below "C" level.

Salesman (in front of house): Little girl, is your mother
   at home?
Little Girl: Yes, sir.
Salesman (after knocking without luck): I thought you
   said your mother was at home?
Little Girl: Yes she is, but I don't live here.

Little Boy (on phone): My mother isn't home.

Caller: How about your father?

Little Boy: Not home either.

Caller: Who is home?

Little Boy: My sister.

Caller: Will you get your sister?

Little Boy: Okay . . . (delay) . . . I'm sorry, but you can't talk to her.

Caller: Why not?

Little Boy: I can't get her out of her crib.

A boy went to the drugstore to buy a can of talcum powder.

The clerk asked, "Do you want it scented?"

The boy answered, "No thanks, I'll take it with me."

Father: Billy, please take the dog out and give him
    some air.

Billy: Okay, Dad. Where is the nearest gas station?

A little boy rushed by a policeman. Five minutes
later he dashed by again. After he had raced by several
times, the policeman stopped him. "What's the idea,
Sonny?" asked the policeman. "Where are you going?"

The boy looked up and said, "I'm running away from
home."

"If you are running away from home, how come
you've gone around the block so many times?"

"It's the best I can do," the little boy said as he sped
off again. "My mother won't let me cross the street."

Horace: Does your dog have fleas?

Morris: Don't be silly. Dogs don't have fleas—they have puppies.

Librarian: Sh-hh-hh! The people next to you can't read.

Student: What a shame! I've been reading ever since I was six years old.

Little Girl (answering phone): Hello!

Voice: Hello, is Boo there?

Little Girl: Boo who?

Voice: Don't cry, little girl. I guess I dialed the wrong number.

A small boy stood in front of the shoemaker's shop watching the man at work.

"What do you fix shoes with, Mister?" he asked.

"Hide," replied the shoemaker.

"What?" asked the boy.

"I said hide," replied the shoemaker impatiently.

"What for?" the boy asked.

"Hide! The cow's outside," the man said.

"I don't care if it is. I'm not afraid of a cow," the young boy replied.

Willie's father took him to the bird house in the zoo. They came to the stork cage. For a long time Willie looked at the stork, then turned at last to his father and sighed:

"Ah, Daddy, he never even recognized me."

Son: I want a choo choo for Christmas.
Mom: A what?
Son: A choo choo. A CHOO CHOO!
Mom: Coming down with a cold?

Doctor: What seems to be the trouble?
Youngster: I swallowed a clock last week.
Doctor: Good grief, this is serious! Why didn't you come to me sooner?
Youngster: I didn't want to alarm anybody.

Sam's mother heard that old Mrs. Jones was ailing. "Sam," she said, "run across the street and ask how old Mrs. Jones is."

"Sure!" said Sam.

A few minutes later Sam came back and said, "Mrs. Jones told me it's none of your business how old she is."

A mother brought her child to school to register him. However, the child was only five and the age required was six.

"I think," the mother said to the principal, "that he can pass the six-year-old test."

"We'll see," replied the principal.

Then to the child, the principal said, "Son, just say a few words that come to your mind."

"Do you want logically connected sentences," asked the child, "or purely irrelevant words?"

Junior: Can you write in the dark, dad?
Dad: I think so. What is it you want me to write?
Junior: Your name on this report card.

All the little pigeons had left the nest and learned to fly but one. The mother pigeon said, "Son, if you don't learn to fly, I'll tow you along behind me."

"No," said the little pigeon. "I'll learn! I don't want to be pigeon-towed!"

Mother: Suzie, have you finished putting the salt into the salt shakers?
Little Suzie: Not yet. It's hard work pushing the salt through all those little holes.

Little Suzie was learning to brush her teeth. She came to her mother and asked, "Mommy, how much toothpaste should I put on my brush?"

"Oh, about the size of a bean," the mother replied.

A little while later Suzie returned with toothpaste spread from cheek to cheek.

Mother shook her head and said, "I told you the size of a bean."

Suzie looked at the brush and back to her mother and said, "Oh, I thought you meant a string bean!"

Mother: Suzie, why are you crying?
Suzie: My dolly—Billie broke it.
Mother: How did he break it?
Suzie: I hit him on the head with it.

Father: Who was that calling?
Junior: No one special, just someone who said it was a long distance from Tokyo and I said it sure was.

Junior: Why does it rain, dad?
Father: To make the flowers grow—and the grass and the trees.
Junior: So why does it rain on the sidewalk?

Mother: Junior, you've been fighting again! You've lost your two front teeth.
Junior: Oh, no I haven't, mother. I have them in my pocket.

Eye Doctor: There now, with these glasses you'll be able to read everything.

Little Boy: You mean, I don't have to go to school anymore?

"Were you nervous about asking your father for a raise in your allowance?"

"No, I was calm and collected."

Mother: What are you drawing, Junior?

Junior: A picture of heaven.

Mother: But you can't do that. No one knows what heaven looks like.

Junior: They will after I've finished.

The telephone rang and little Suzie answered. It was her girlfriend.

"Can you call back in around fifteen minutes?" said little Suzie. "I can't talk now, I'm in the middle of a tantrum."

A three-year-old had received a severe sunburn which reached the peeling stage. His mother heard him saying to himself as he was washing up for dinner, "Only three years old and wearing out already."

3 Zanies

Nit: Can you telephone from an airplane?
Wit: Sure, anyone can tell a phone from an airplane. The plane is the one without the dial tone.

Ernie: There's a man outside with a wooden leg named Smith.
Bernie: What's the name of his other leg?

Nit: I just had ten rides on the carousel.
Wit: You really do get around, don't you?

Lem: That star over there is Mars.
Clem: Then that other one must be Pa's.

"Hello."
"Hello."
"Is that you, Sam?"
"This is Sam, speaking."
"Are you sure this is Sam?"
"Certainly this is Sam."
"Well, listen Sam. This is Joe. Lend me fifty dollars."
"I'll tell Sam when he comes in."

A man's car motor went dead as he was driving along a country road. He stepped out of his car to see if he could fix it.

A big cow came along and stopped beside him. She took a look at the motor and said, "Your trouble is probably in the carburetor." Startled, the man jumped back and ran down the road until he met a farmer walking. He told the farmer what had happened.

The farmer asked, "Does the cow have a big brown-and-white spot over her left eye?"

"Yes, yes!" cried the motorist.

"Oh, don't pay attention to Old Bossy. She doesn't know a thing about cars."

Nit: I know a restaurant where we can eat dirt cheap.
Wit: Who wants to eat dirt?

Moe: Have you had your dinner yet?
Joe: Yes. I was so hungry at seven fifty-nine that I eight o'clock.

Ike: What are all those chickens doing out in front of your house?
Mike: They heard I was going to lay some bricks and they want to see how it's done.

City Boy: Look at that bunch of cows.
Farm Boy: Not bunch, herd.
City Boy: Heard what?
Farm Boy: Of cows.
City Boy: Sure, I've heard of cows.
Farm Boy: No, I mean a cow herd.
City Boy: I don't care. I have no secrets from them.

A big mean lion was walking through the jungle. The first animal he met was a monkey. The lion pounced on the poor monkey and asked, "Who is the king of the jungle?" The frightened monkey replied, "You are, O mighty lion!" So the lion let him go.

The next animal the lion met was a zebra. He pounced on the zebra and roared, "Who is the king of the jungle?" The frightened zebra replied, "You are, O mighty lion!" So the lion let him go.

The lion walked on until he met an elephant and asked the same question. The elephant grabbed the lion, twirled him around, and threw him fifty feet.

The lion picked himself off the ground. "Just because you don't know the answer is no reason for you to get rough."

Dit: What is the best way to mount a horse?
Dot: How should I know? I'm no taxidermist.

Joe: My aunt collects fleas for a living.
Moe: What does your uncle do?
Joe: Scratch.

A hillbilly and his son were sitting in front of the fire smoking their pipes, crossing and uncrossing their legs. After a long silence, the father said, "Son, step outside and see if it's raining."

Without looking up, the son answered, "Aw, Pop, why don't we just call in the dog and see if he's wet?"

Ding: They laughed when Bell invented the steamboat.
Dong: That goes to show you how much you know. Fulton invented the steamboat.
Ding: No wonder they laughed.

Patient: My stomach's been aching ever since I ate those twelve oysters yesterday.
Doctor: Were they fresh?
Patient: I don't know.
Doctor: Well, how did they look when you opened the shells?
Patient: You're supposed to open the shells?

Farmer Smith: Do you like raisin bread?
Farmer Jones: Can't say. Never raised any.

Nit: Should you eat fried chicken with your fingers?
Wit: No, you should eat your fingers separately.

Moe: What are you reading?
Joe: I'm reading about electricity.
Moe: Current events?
Joe: No, light reading.

Farmer: This is a dogwood tree.
City Man: How can you tell?
Farmer: By its bark.

Sam: My puppy has a pedigree.
Pam: Do you have papers for it?
Sam: Of course, all over the house.

Ernie: I can't believe my eyes! There's a dog on Main
   Street handing out parking tickets.
Bernie: Is it a brown dog with pointy ears and a long
   tail?
Ernie: Yes, it is.
Bernie: Well, no wonder, that's the town police dog!

A man walked up to the delivery window at the post office, where a new clerk was sorting mail.

"Any mail for Mike Howe?" the man asked.

The clerk ignored him, and the man repeated the question in a louder voice. Without looking up, the clerk replied, "No, none for your cow, and none for your horse either!"

Passenger: Is this my train?
Conductor: No sir, it belongs to the railroad company.
Passenger: Don't be funny! Can I take this train to Boston?
Conductor: No sir, it's much too heavy.

Sheriff to Cowboy: Quick—did you see which way the computer programmer went?

Cowboy: He went data way!

First Vampire: A panhandler came up to me yesterday and told me he hadn't had a bite in days.

Second Vampire: So what did you do?

First Vampire: What could I do? I bit him.

Customer: I'd like to buy some steak, but make it lean, please.

Butcher: Which way do you want it to lean, right or left?

"What's one and one?"

"Two."

"What's four minus two?"

"Two."

"Who wrote Tom Sawyer?"

"Twain."

"Now say all the answers together."

"Two, two Twain."

"Have a nice twip!"

Tutti: I can't sleep, what shall I do?

Frutti: Lie near the edge of the bed, and you'll drop right off.

Have you ever stopped to wonder why goods sent by ship is called cargo, but goods sent by car is a shipment?

Patient: Doctor, I need help.

Psychiatrist: What's the problem?

Patient: I think I'm a dog.

Psychiatrist: Please come into my office and lie down on the couch.

Patient: I can't. I'm not allowed on the furniture.

Bob: I know the capital of North Carolina.

Ray: Really?

Bob: No, Raleigh.

Waiter: Would you like a hero sandwich?

Customer: No, thanks, I'm the chicken type myself.

Tip: You can't drive that nail into the wall with a hairbrush.

Top: Really?

Tip: Of course, use your head.

A customer entered a music store and asked the sales clerk if he carried pianos.

"Not if I can get out of it," the clerk replied. "I'm not strong enough."

Wise man says:

Bird in hand makes it hard to blow nose.

Mother: You're cleaning up the spilled coffee with cake?

Daughter: Of course, Mother. It's sponge cake.

Boy: Where were you when the parade went by?
Girl: I was home waving my hair.
Boy: That's stupid, next time use a flag.

Nit: Where shall we meet?
Wit: Under the clothesline.
Nit: Why under the clothesline?
Wit: That's where I hang out.

Sue: I found a horseshoe.

Lou: Do you know that means good luck?

Sue: It may be good luck for me, but some poor horse is running around in his stocking feet.

Lem: What are you doing?

Clem: I'm painting a picture of a cow eating grass.

Lem: Where is the grass?

Clem: The cow ate it.

Lem: Where is the cow?

Clem: The cow left. Why should it hang around after all the grass is gone?

Caller (on phone): Hello? Is this the Weather Bureau?

Weather Bureau: Yes, it is.

Caller: How about a shower tonight?

Weather Bureau: It's all right with us. Take one if you need one.

Juliet (to Romeo): "If you had gotten orchestra seats like I asked you, I wouldn't be up on this balcony.

Lem: I had a terrible nightmare last night.

Clem: What did you dream about?

Lem: I dreamt I was eating Shredded Wheat.

Clem: Why should that upset you?

Lem: When I woke up, half the mattress was gone.

Izzy: Did you hear the big noise this morning?

Dizzy: No. What was it, the crack of dawn?

Izzy: Nope, it was the break of day.

Dit: Did you know that the way my room is arranged, I can lie in bed and watch the sun rise?

Dot: That's nothing. I can sit in my living room and watch the kitchen sink.

Lady (in paint store): Do you have any wallpaper with flowers in it?

Clerk: Yes, we do.

Lady: Can I put it on myself?

Clerk: Of course, if you like, but it would look better on the wall.

Sue: I just came from a big fire sale.
Lou: What did you buy?
Sue: Four big fires.

A man waiting for a bus held his hands about four inches apart. He got on the bus, and when the driver asked for his fare, the man told him to take the money out of his coat pocket. The driver did as he said and drove on.

The man walked to the rear of the bus and sat down, still holding his hands in the same position. A woman passenger turned to him and asked, "Were you wounded in the war?"

"No, I wasn't," he replied.

"Then why are you holding your hands like that?"

"Because I'm on my way to a hardware store and I need a piece of pipe this long."

Fuzzie: Want to hear a couple of dillies?
Wuzzie: Sure!
Fuzzie: Dilly, dilly.

Mutt: Hello?
   —You don't say!
   —You don't say! (he hangs up).
Jeff: Who was that?
Mutt: He didn't say.

Tutti: May I sit on your right hand?
Frutti: You can for a while, but I may need it later to eat with.

Lem: You play chess with your dog? He must be very smart.

Clem: Not really. I beat him most of the time.

Dog Owner: I'm worried, Doc. What should I do if my dog has ticks?

Veterinarian: Don't wind him.

Moe: That's a mighty strange-looking dog.

Joe: He's a genuine police dog.

Moe: He doesn't look like any police dog I've ever seen.

Joe: Of course not. He's in the secret service.

A woman telephoned an airline office in New York and asked, "How long does it take to fly to Boston?"

The clerk said, "Just a minute."

"Thank you," the woman said as she hung up.

Flip: Every night I dream I'm flying.

Flop: Why don't you sleep on your back?

Flip: What? And fly upside down?

The thunder god went for a ride on his favorite filly.

"I'm Thor!" he cried.

The horse answered, "You forgot the thaddle, thilly."

Lem: Where is the park?

Clem: There isn't any here.

Lem: Then how come the sign says, "Park Here"?

Ding: Why are you taking your ruler to bed with you?

Dong: To see how long I sleep.

Mutt: My feet are frozen and they're sticking out of the covers.

Jeff: You fool! Why don't you pull them in?

Mutt: Oh, no! I'm not putting those cold things in bed with me.

Sam: I snored so loud that I used to wake myself up. But I finally cured myself.

Pam: How did you do that?

Sam: Now I sleep in the next room.

Tip: What's a football made of?

Top: Pig's hide.

Tip: Why should they hide?

Top: No. The pig's outside.

Tip: Well bring him in. Any friend of yours is a friend of mine.

A world traveler was lecturing the club about his adventures.

"There are some spectacles," he said, "that one never forgets."

"I wish you could get me a pair," one member of the club said. "I'm always forgetting mine."

A lady went to a pet shop to buy a sweater for her dog. The clerk asked for the shape and size of the dog. However, the lady could not describe the dog accurately.

"Why don't you bring the dog in so I can fit him properly?" the clerk asked.

"Oh, I couldn't do that," the lady replied, "I want it to be a surprise."

A dog was so clever, his owner sent him to college. Home for vacation, the dog admitted he had learned neither history nor science, but added proudly, "I did make a good start in foreign languages."

"Okay," replied the owner, "say something in a foreign language."

The dog said, "Meow!"

Ding: I lost my dog.
Dong: Why don't you put an ad in the paper?
Ding: What good would that do? He can't read.

Iggy: When I sneeze, I put my hand in front of my mouth.
Ziggy: Why do you do that?
Iggy: To catch my teeth.

Fuzzy: Last night I put my tooth under my pillow. This morning I found a dime there instead.
Wuzzy: When I put mine under my pillow, I got a dollar.
Fuzzy: Well, you have buck teeth.

Reporter (interviewing famous matador): Is it true that the bull becomes irritated when you wave your red cape at him?

Matador: Actually, the cows are the ones. The reason a bull gets mad at the red cape is because he doesn't like being mistaken for a cow.

Ike: Why are you sleeping under that old car?
Mike: So I can wake up oily in the morning.

Mutt: I wish I were in your shoes.
Jeff: Why would you want to be in my shoes?
Mutt: Mine have holes in them.

A formation of geese was flying south for the winter. One of the geese in the rear said to another: "How come we always have to follow that same leader?"

"He's the one with the map," the other replied.

"One man's Mede is another man's Persian."
"Are you Shah?"
"Sultanly."

Nit: What was the tow truck doing at the race track?
Wit: Trying to pull a fast one.

Newlywed Wife: I baked two kinds of biscuits today, dear. Would you like to take your pick?
Husband: No, thank you. I'll just use the hammer.

Nit: I just flew in from Europe.
Wit: I bet your arms are tired.

Lem: I just sat down on a pin.
Clem: Did it hurt?
Lem: No, it was a safety pin.

Horace: What are you doing?
Morris: I'm drawing my bath.
Horace: I paint a little myself.

Girl: I'd like a triple vanilla ice cream sundae with chocolate syrup, nuts, and lots of whipped cream.
Waiter: With a cherry on top?
Girl: Heavens no! I'm on a diet.

Nita: Did you hear about the girl who went on a coconut diet?
Rita: Did she lose weight?
Nita: Not a pound, but you should see her climb trees!

Tutti: English food must be fattening.
Frutti: Whatever gave you that idea?
Tutti: I read in the paper about a woman in London who lost five hundred pounds.

Mr. Monster woke at midnight in a terrible temper. "Where's my supper?" he yelled at his wife. "Where are my chains? Where is my poison? Where is my . . .?"

"Now wait a minute," Mrs. Monster replied. "Can't you see I only have three hands?"

The two boys were boasting.

First Boy: You know the Panama Canal? Well, my father dug the hole for it.

Second Boy: You know the Dead Sea? Well, my father killed it.

Biff: London is the foggiest place in the world.

Boff: Oh, no it isn't. I've been in a place much foggier than London.

Biff: Where was that?

Boff: I don't know, it was too foggy to tell.

Flip: What happened to your car? It's all banged up!

Flop: I was out driving and hit a cow.

Flip: A Jersey?

Flop: I don't know. I didn't get its license.

Igor: Why do you call your pet fawn "Ninety-Nine Cents"?

Boris: Because it's not old enough to be a buck.

Mutt: How much money do you have with you?

Jeff: Oh, between $48 and $50.

Mutt: Isn't that a lot of money to be carrying around?

Mutt: No, $2 isn't much.

Customer: Waiter! I just found this hair in my turtle soup.

Waiter: Well, well! So the turtle and the hare finally did get together.

Doctor: Ever had an accident?

Farmer: No.

Doctor: Never had an accident in your whole life?

Farmer: Well, last spring I was out in the field and the bull tossed me over the fence.

Doctor: Don't you call that an accident?

Farmer: No, the bull did it on purpose.

First Farmer: My scarecrow is so natural that it frightened every crow off the farm.

Second Farmer: That's nothing. The one on our farm scared the crows so much, they brought back all the corn they stole last year.

Ike: This match won't light.
Mike: What's the matter with it?
Ike: I don't really know—it lit before.

A fisherman carrying a lobster bumped into a friend on the way home.

"Where are you going with the lobster under your arm?" asked his friend.

The fisherman answered, "I'm taking him home to dinner."

Just then the lobster spoke up: "I've already had my dinner. Can we go to a movie instead?"

A lady was invited to a costume party. She went to a store to rent a costume. The manager of the store showed her a beautiful princess costume with gown, lovely shoes and a crown.

The lady asked, "How much?"

The manager said, "Twenty dollars."

The lady hadn't expected to spend that much, so she asked to see something cheaper.

Next the manager brought out a plain dress.

"How much?" the lady asked.

"Ten dollars," the manager replied.

This was still more than she expected to pay.

By this time the manager was becoming impatient. "I have the perfect thing for you," he said. "For one dollar, I'll give you a broomstick and a can of red paint."

"That sounds reasonable to me," said the lady, "but what do I do with it?"

"Stick the broomstick in your mouth," answered the manager, "pour the red paint all over your head, and go as a jelly apple."

Beggar: I haven't had more than one meal a day all week, lady.

Fat Lady: Oh, how I wish I had your will power!

Dit: Peculiar, isn't it?

Dot: What is peculiar?

Dit: A person can walk a mile without moving more than two feet.

Flip: Are your blinds drawn?
Flop: No, they're real blinds.

It was the man's first trip by airplane. He was frightened and nervous. As the engines began to roar, he gripped the arms of his seat, closed his eyes, and counted to one hundred.

When he opened his eyes he looked out of the window. "See those tiny people down there," he said to the woman sitting next to him, "don't they look like ants?"

"They are ants," the woman said. "We haven't left the ground yet."

Ned: Did I ever tell you about the time I came face to face with a ferocious lion?
Fred: No, what happened?
Ned: There I stood alone, without a gun. The lion crept closer and closer and closer . . .
Fred: Then what did you do?
Ned: What could I do? I moved on to the next cage.

Moe: I've been seeing spots before my eyes lately.
Joe: Have you seen a doctor?
Moe: No, just spots.

Patient: Doctor, I haven't been able to sleep for a week. Every night I dream of a door with a sign on it. I push and I push—but I still can't open it.
Doctor: What does the sign say?
Patient: "Pull."

An accountant got out of bed one morning and complained that he had not slept a wink.

"Why didn't you count sheep?" his wife asked.

"I did, and that's what got me into trouble," the accountant replied. "I made a mistake during the first hour, and it took until this morning to correct it."

Flora: My husband has dreadful table manners. He always holds his little pinky out when he holds a cup of tea.

Dora: In society it is considered polite to hold out your little pinky when drinking tea.

Flora: With the teabag hanging from it?

A cowboy was leading a flock of sheep down Main Street when he was ordered to stop by the town policeman.

"What's wrong?" the cowboy asked. "I was just heading my ewes into a side street."

"That's the trouble," the policeman replied. "No ewe turns permitted on Main Street."

A cowboy was riding his horse when he saw a little dog running down the road.

"Hi!" said the dog.

"Hi!" replied the surprised cowboy. "I didn't know dogs could talk."

His horse turned his head and said, "You learn something new every day, don't you?"

A husband brought his wife to the doctor.

Husband: My wife thinks she's a chicken.

Doctor: That's terrible. How long has she been this way?

Husband: For three years.

Doctor: Why didn't you bring her to see me sooner?

Husband: We needed the eggs.

Tutti: Did you see me when I passed by?

Frutti: Yes, I did.

Tutti: You never saw me before in your life, did you?

Frutti: I don't think so.

Tutti: Then how did you know it was me?

A mouse was dancing madly on top of a jar of jam. Another mouse came along and asked him why he was dancing.

"Can't you read?" replied the first mouse. "It says, 'Twist to Open'."

A man bought a mousetrap. When he brought it home, he discovered that he had no cheese to bait it with. So he found a picture of some cheese, and put the picture in the trap.

The next morning he went to the trap to see if it had caught anything. The picture of the cheese was gone. In its place was a picture of a mouse.

Mrs. Jones: Is your house warm?

Mrs. Smith: It should be—the painters gave it three coats last week.

Dit: A snake just snapped at me.

Dot: Don't be silly. Snakes don't snap.

Dit: This one did, it was a garter snake.

A man was sitting on his porch rocking back and forth. He seemed to be having a long discussion with himself. Every once in a while he broke into loud laughter. At other times, he shouted "Phooey" in disgust.

A policeman passing by stopped to watch the man and asked him what was going on. "I'm telling myself jokes," the man told him. "And if I say so myself, most of them are very funny."

"Then why do you keep saying 'phooey'?" the policeman asked.

"I only say that when I heard 'em before."

Biff: Can you tell me what time it is? I was invited to a birthday party and my watch isn't going.

Boff: Why? Wasn't your watch invited?

4 That's Entertainment!

Mr. Magic: I can turn this handkerchief into a flower.

Little Boy: That's nothing. I can walk down the street and turn into an alley.

A magician finished eating a rabbit stew and rushed out of the restaurant saying to the waiter, "That rabbit stew made me sick!"

The waiter, looking at him run, said, "Well, that must be the first time a rabbit ever made a magician disappear."

Interviewer: Tell me, Ali Baba, what is it like, flying on a magic carpet?

Ali Baba: Rugged.

Customer (at carnival): That knife-throwing act was terrible. I want my money back.

Carnival Owner: What was the matter with it?

Customer: Call that a knife-thrower? He got 10 chances and he didn't even hit that girl once!

A magician performed his magic act on a luxury ship every evening. Also on board the ship was a parrot which belonged to one of the sailors. Every time the magician went into his act, the parrot screamed, "Phony! Phony!"

One day the ship sank. All that was left was the parrot sitting on one end of a log and the magician on the other end. The parrot turned to the magician and said, "Okay, wise guy, what did you do with the ship?"

The most popular sideshow in the circus was a horse that played jazz piano.

A farmer who saw the show was amazed. He asked the horse's trainer how the horse learned to play.

"No mystery," the trainer explained, "he took lessons for years."

Ike: Did you hear what happened at the flea circus?
Mike: No, what happened?
Ike: A dog came along and stole the show.

Newspaper headline:
Local Man Takes First Prize in Dog Show.

On their way to the seashore for a weekend engagement, a trainer and his talking dog were speeding along in a new sports car when a police car started closing in on them.

"Better pull up to the side of the road," the dog told the trainer. "And remember—when he gets here, let me do the talking!"

Did you hear about the French horn player whose toupee fell into his instrument? He spent the rest of the concert blowing his top.

Dit: Do you know what the elephant rock-'n-roll star said into the microphone?
Dot: No, what?
Dit: Tusking—one two three; tusking—one two three.

Ernie: My uncle can play the piano by ear.
Bernie: That's nothing. My uncle can fiddle with his whiskers.

Teacher: Where is the English Channel?
Pupil: I don't know. Our TV set only picks up local stations.

A dog walked into a theatrical agent's office carrying a small case. The dog asked for an audition. "Okay, let's see your act," the agent said.

The dog opened the case and out flew a butterfly who sang "The Star-Spangled Banner" in a rich baritone voice.

The theatrical agent was astonished. He promptly signed the act.

Five minutes later, the dog returned. "I have a confession to make," the dog began. "I was not truthful with you and my conscience is bothering me. The butterfly did not actually sing 'The Star-Spangled Banner'. You see, I'm a ventriloquist."

The actor came into the agent's office and said, "My act is really different. I can fly."

He then flew up to the ceiling, circled the room a few times, and came down in a perfect landing.

The agent was not impressed. "Okay," he said, "so you can imitate birds. But what else can you do?"

Dancer: Can you stretch the music out a little longer?
Orchestra Leader: Sorry, but this isn't a rubber band.

Ned: What did you get the little medal for?
Fred: For singing.
Ned: What did you get the big medal for?
Fred: For stopping.

Did you hear about the new dance called the Elevator? It has no steps.

Did you hear about the composer who took too many baths? He began to write soap operas.

Sam was playing the piano for his friend Paul.
"Well, how do you like it?" Sam asked.
"I wish you were on radio," Paul replied.
"You mean I'm that good."
"No," Paul said, "because then I could turn you off."

At the end of a bad piano concert, the pianist proudly remarked that he played everything by ear. A member of the audience remarked, "That explains it. I didn't think those sounds could be made by human hands."

Then there was the classical pianist who was not a good speller. When she went out to buy something she left a sign on the door which said, "Out Chopin. Be Bach in a minuet."

Sign in a music store window:

GUITARS FOR SALE, CHEAP
NO STRINGS ATTACHED

First Monster: Are the monsters in your town ugly?
Second Monster: Oh yes. We held a beauty contest last year and nobody won.

Did you hear about the sword swallower who went on a diet? He was on pins and needles for six months.

Mutt: I was operated on last week and I really enjoyed it.
Jeff: How come?
Mutt: The doctor had me in stitches.

This was the actor's first big film role. In one scene he had to jump from a cliff a hundred feet high into shallow water. The actor took one look at the cliff and the water and refused to make the jump.

"What's the matter?" the director asked.

"I can't jump from that cliff," the actor insisted. "Do you realize there's only one foot of water at the bottom of the cliff?"

"Of course," the director explained. "You think we want you to drown?"

Announcer on TV horror theatre:
    "The Invisible Man will not be seen tonight."

Dit: Whatever happened to the lady you used to saw in half?
Mr. Magic: Oh, she's fine. She lives in San Francisco and New York.

Zip: Did you hear about the sword swallower who swallowed an umbrella?
Zap: No, why did he do that?
Zip: He wanted to put something away for a rainy day.

Arthur thought he was a great comedian. He was always looking for people who would listen to his jokes. The only trouble was that his jokes were awful.

One day Arthur was riding on a bus. A man got on and took a seat next to him.

"Want to hear some great jokes?" Arthur asked. The man said he didn't mind.

After fifteen minutes of the worst jokes he had ever heard in his life, the man asked Arthur if he made up the jokes all by himself.

"Absolutely," replied Arthur. "Out of my head."

"You must be," the man said as he got off the bus.

Lem: The last time I sang, my voice fell on a thousand ears.
Clem: Where were you singing, in a cornfield?

Actor: Have you seen me on television?
Acquaintance: Oh sure, I've seen you on and off.
Actor: How did you like me?
Acquaintance: Off.

Dick: I once sang for the King of Siam. At least that's what he told me he was.
Jane: Really?
Dick: Yes, he said, "If you're a singer, then I'm the King of Siam."

Sign on house: DRUMS FOR SALE.
Sign on house next door: HOORAY!

A trumpet player was blasting away in his apartment late one night. There was a knock on the door. He opened it and there stood his angry next-door neighbor.

"Do you know it is late and I have to get up early tomorrow?"

"No, I don't," the trumpet player said, "but if you can hum a few bars, I can fake the rest."

A goat was in the garbage dump looking for food. He discovered a can of film and promptly ate it. Another goat came along and asked if the film was any good.

"It was all right," the first goat replied. "But personally, I liked the book better."

"How was that science fiction movie you saw?"

"You know, same old thing—boy meets girl—boy loses girl—boy builds new girl."

Ike and Mike went to the movies to see a film about horse racing. Ike said to Mike, "I'll bet you five dollars that number four will win the race." Mike agreed to the bet.

The horse won. But Ike said, "I can't take your money. I have to admit something—I saw the movie yesterday."

"So did I," said Mike, "but I didn't think he could win twice in a row."

A father took his young son to the opera for the first time. The conductor waved his baton and the soprano began to sing. The boy watched everything with interest and finally spoke up. "Why is the conductor hitting her with the stick?"

The father smiled and said, "He's not hitting her."

"Well," asked the boy, "why is she screaming?"

A baby rabbit kept pestering its mother. "Where did I come from, Mom? Huh? Huh? Where did I come from?"

The baby rabbit nagged until its mother finally said, "Stop bothering me, Junior. If you must know, you were pulled out of a magician's hat."

Small Boy: Mr. Magic, could you pull a rabbit out of your hat?

Mr. Magic: I'd love to, my boy, but I just washed my hare, and I can't do a thing with it.

Commercial:

Our product comes in two convenient sizes: 49¢ for the handy pint bottle and $2,000 for the large economy tank car.

Commercial:

Mother's Dill Pickles are untouched by human hands! You are probably wondering how she cuts them and stuffs them into the jars. Well, she has the longest and sharpest toenails you ever saw.

"Step right up, ladies and gentlemen!" the medicine man at the carnival shouted. "I have in this bottle a miraculous fluid which I guarantee will help you live a long and healthy life. To look at me, you would never guess that I am over two hundred years old, would you? Know why I've lived this long? It's because I take a dose of this medicine every day."

A farmer thought he might give the medicine a try, but when he heard it cost five dollars a bottle, he hesitated. He got the medicine man's assistant aside and asked him if it were true that the medicine man was over 200 years old.

"To tell you the truth, I don't know," said the assistant. "I've only been with him for the last 120 years."

Radio Program:
Now for your morning exercises ... Ready? ... Up, down, up, down, up, down ... Now the other eyelid. ...

Commercial:
Have you heard about the new breakfast food for mothers? Instead of going "Snap, Crackle, Pop!" it goes "Snap, Crackle, Mom!"

The teacher asked his pupils to choose books on which to write a brief review. One lad chose the phone book. He wrote on his report: "This book hasn't got much of a plot, but boy, what a cast!"

Agent (to writer): I've got some good news and some
   bad news.
Writer: First tell me the good news.
Agent: Paramount just loved your story, absolutely ate
   it up.
Writer: That's fantastic. And the bad news?
Agent: Paramount is my dog.

Horace: What kind of dog is that?
Morris: That's a bird dog.
Horace: Funny, I never heard him sing.

The chief of police in the small town was scolding his not-too-bright deputy.

"But how could you let the robber get away from you in broad daylight?"

"Chief, I couldn't help it. The robber ran into a movie theatre."

"Why didn't you run after him?" the Chief asked angrily.

"I would have, Chief, but I'd already seen the movie."

The movie was at a dramatic moment when a woman was disturbed by an old man looking for something on the floor.

"What have you lost?" the woman asked in an irritated voice.

"A caramel," the old man replied.

"A caramel!" she said. "Do you mean to say that you are disturbing me and everyone else for a caramel?"

"Yes," the old man explained and continued to look. "My teeth are in it."

"Pardon me, lady," the young man said in the darkness of the movie house. "Did I step on your toes a moment ago?"

"You certainly did," the woman on the aisle said.

"Good, then I'm in the right row," the young man said as he went back to his seat.

5 Unfriendly Advice

A pesty child was making more and more of a nuisance of himself by playing ball in the aisle of an airplane. One man was particularly annoyed and finally lost his temper.

"Listen, kid," he said. "Why don't you go outside and play?"

Sign on newly seeded lawn:
   DOGS BEWARE, VICIOUS MAN!

Patient: Doctor, I get the feeling that people don't give a hoot about anything I say.
Psychiatrist: So?

Mother (on phone): Doctor, doctor! Junior has swallowed a bullet. What should I do?
Doctor: Don't point him at anybody.

Doctor: What is the problem?
Patient: I swallowed a roll of film.
Doctor: Don't worry, nothing serious will develop.

Customer: I have a complaint.

Waiter: A complaint? This is a restaurant, not a hospital.

Three boys walked into a candy store. The first one said, "I want a dime's worth of jelly beans."

It happened that the jelly beans were way up on the top shelf. The old storekeeper had to get a ladder and climb up, bring down the jar, count out ten cents worth of jelly beans, climb up and put the jar back. Then the storekeeper climbed down, put the ladder away and turned to the second boy.

"I want a dime's worth of jelly beans, too," said the boy.

So the old man got the ladder, climbed up and brought down the jar, counted out another dime's worth of jelly beans. However, before he put the jar back, he had a thought. He said to the third boy: "Do you want a dime's worth of jelly beans, too?

"No," the boy replied.

So the old man climbed up, returned the jar, climbed down, put the ladder away, and came back to the counter.

"Now," he said to the third boy, "what can I do for you?"

"I want a nickel's worth of jelly beans."

Teacher: Sam, what is the outside of a tree called?
Sam: I don't know.
Teacher: Bark, Sam, bark.
Sam: Bow, wow, wow!

A man was having trouble with a gopher in his yard. He went to the exterminator and asked how to get rid of the pest. The exterminator said, "I'd recommend the four-day process." The homeowner had never heard of this process and asked how it worked.

"Simple," said the exterminator. "Every morning at seven you drop an apple and a cookie down the gopher hole. But at seven in the morning on the fourth day, you just drop in an apple. You wait five, ten, maybe fifteen minutes. All of a sudden the gopher will pop up, and when he asks, 'Where's the cookie?', you clobber him."

"Mommy, all the kids say I look like a werewolf."
"Shut up and comb your face!"

Mrs. Jones: I'm sorry to bother you on such a terrible night, doctor.

Doctor: That's all right. I had another patient down the road, so I thought I'd kill two birds with one stone.

Customer: Waiter, there is a fly in this ice cream.

Waiter: Serves him right. Let him freeze!

Slavemaster to Roman galley slaves who have been pulling on oars for hours:

I have some good news for you and some bad news. The good news is: you can have 15 minutes rest. Now for the bad news: At the end of the rest period, the captain wants to go water-skiing.

First Rancher: What's the name of your place?

Second Rancher: The XWK Lazy R Double Diamond Circle Q Bar S.

First Rancher: How many heads of cattle do you have?

Second Rancher: Only a few. Not many survive the branding.

Doctor: Ouch! OUCH!

Mother: Junior, please say "ah" so the nice doctor can take his finger out of your mouth.

The mother ran into the nursery when she heard her five-year-old son howling. His baby sister had been pulling his hair.

"Don't mind the baby," his mother said. "She doesn't know that it hurts you."

A few minutes later, the mother ran back to the nursery. This time it was the baby doing the screaming.

"What's the matter with the baby?" the mother asked.

"Nothing much," her five-year-old son replied, "but now she knows."

Insurance Salesman: You really should buy our accident insurance policy.

Customer: Why should I?

Insurance Salesman: Just last week I sold an accident insurance policy to a man. The next day he broke his neck and we paid out $50,000. Just think, you might be as lucky as he was!

Mother: How do you like your new teacher?

Little Girl: I don't like her very much.

Mother: Why not?

Little Girl: She told me to sit up front for the present—and then she didn't give me a present.

Father: Junior, I see by your report card that you are not doing well in history. How come?

Junior: I can't help it. The teacher always asks me about things that happened before I was born.

Teacher: Why are you crawling into class, Arthur?

Arthur: Because class has already started and you said, "Don't anyone dare walk into my class late!"

Doctor: How do you feel today?

Patient: Very much better, thank you. The only thing still bothering me is my breathing.

Doctor: We'll try to find something to stop that.

Horace: That is a beautiful stuffed lion you have there. Where did you get him?

Morris: In Africa, when I was on a hunting expedition with my uncle.

Horace: What is he stuffed with?

Morris: My uncle.

Tip: Did I ever tell you the story about my forebears?

Top: No, but I've heard the one about the three bears.

Silly: What is the best way to clean a tuba?
Sillier: With a tuba toothpaste.

Sign in a pet shop window:
BOXER PUPPY FOR SALE. HOUSEBROKEN, FAITHFUL, WILL EAT ANYTHING. ESPECIALLY FOND OF CHILDREN.

First Invisible Man: Did you miss me when I was gone?
Second Invisible Man: Were you gone?

6 Truth Is
Stranger Than . . .

Teacher: Let us take the example of the busy ant. He works all the time, night and day. Then what happens?
Pupil: He gets stepped on.

Tutti: He was once a lord who owned many castles. When he gave them up, he became very rude.
Frutti: Would you say he lost all his manors?

The dentist walked up to his patient, who let out a wild scream.

"What are you hollering for?" the dentist asked. "You're not even in the chair yet."

"I know, doc," the patient answered, "but you're stepping on my corn."

Ned: I just burned a hundred dollar bill.
Fred: Wow! You must be rich.
Ned: Not really. It was a bill from my dentist.

A family that had spent its vacation on a farm the year before wished to return again. The only thing wrong with the farm was the noise the pigs made.

The family wrote to the farmer to ask if the pigs were still there. The farmer wrote back, "Don't worry. We haven't had pigs on the farm since you were here."

Flim: I paid a hundred dollars for that dog—part collie and part bull.
Flam: Which part is bull?
Flim: The part about the hundred dollars.

Harry: Didn't you say your dog's bark was worse than his bite?
Larry: Yes I did.
Harry: Then for goodness sake, don't let him bark. He just bit me.

Lem: Don't be afraid. This dog will eat off your hand.
Clem: That's exactly what I'm afraid of.

Teacher: Where is your pencil, Harold?
Harold: I ain't got none.
Teacher: How many times have I told you not to say that, Harold? Now listen: I do not have a pencil, you do not have a pencil, they do not have a pencil ... Now, Harold, do you understand?
Harold: Not really. What happened to all the pencils?

A horse walked into a soda fountain and ordered an ice cream sundae with chocolate ice cream and strawberry syrup, sprinkled with nuts.

The young man behind the counter brought the sundae to the horse, who finished it off with great pleasure.

Noticing how the young man stared at him as he ate, the horse said, "I suppose you think it strange that a horse should come into a soda fountain and order a sundae with chocolate ice cream and strawberry syrup, sprinkled with nuts?"

"Not at all," the young man replied. "I like it that way myself."

Irv: What are you up to?
Merv: I'm writing a letter to myself.
Irv: What does it say?
Merv: I don't know. I won't get it until tomorrow.

Nita: The trouble with you is you're always wishing for something you don't have.
Rita: Well, what else is there to wish for?

Lem: Did you hear about the turtle on the New Jersey Turnpike?
Clem: What was the turtle doing on the turnpike?
Lem: About one mile an hour.

Teacher (correcting a pupil): When I asked you what shape the world was in, I meant "round" or "flat"—not "rotten."

First Mouse: I finally got that scientist trained.

Second Mouse: How so?

First Mouse: Every time I go through that maze and ring the bell, he gives me something to eat.

Teacher: If you add 3,462 and 3,096, then divide the answer by 4, and then multiply by 6, what would you get?

Melvin: The wrong answer.

Teacher: Are you good in arithmetic?

Pupil: Yes and no.

Teacher: What does that mean?

Pupil: Yes, I'm no good in arithmetic.

A family of bears feeding in Yellowstone Park looked up as a car crammed with eight tourists pulled up to the side of the road.

"It's cruel," Papa Bear said to his family, "to keep them caged up like that!"

A baby bear was born in the zoo yesterday and who do you think they sent to cover the story? A cub reporter.

Do Smokey the Bear posters help? Of course they do! Ever since they started putting Smokey the Bear posters in the New York City subways, there hasn't been a single forest fire in Manhattan.

Dit: I know a woman who is black and blue because she puts on cold cream, face cream, wrinkle cream, vanishing cream, hand cream, and skin cream every night.
Dot: Why would that make her black and blue?
Dit: All night long she keeps on slipping out of bed.

Customer: And this, I suppose, is one of those hideous things you call modern art?
Art Dealer: No, it's a mirror.

The teacher asked the class to write a composition telling what they would do if they had a million dollars.

Every pupil except Little Audrey began to write immediately. Little Audrey sat idle, twiddling her thumbs, looking out the window.

Teacher collected the papers, and Little Audrey handed in a blank sheet.

"Why Audrey," teacher said, "everyone has written two pages or more, while you have done nothing. Why is that?"

"Well," replied Little Audrey, "that's what I would do if I had a million dollars."

Boy on hands and knees looking for something.
Man: What are you looking for, young man?
Boy: I lost a dollar and I can't find it.
Man: Don't worry, you will. A dollar doesn't go very far these days.

Tourist: The flies are awfully thick around here. Don't
  you people ever shoo them?
Native: Nope, we just let them go barefoot.

His teen-age daughter had been on the phone for half
an hour. When she finally hung up, her father said,
"Usually you are on the phone for at least two hours.
How come this time the conversation was so short?"
  "Wrong number," the daughter replied.

Customer: Waiter, this meat is bad.
Waiter: Who told you?
Customer: A little swallow.

Customer: Waiter, this coffee tastes like mud.
Waiter: Of course it does, it was freshly ground.

Teacher: How old were you on your last birthday?
Pupil: Seven.
Teacher: How old will you be on your next birthday?
Pupil: Nine.
Teacher: That's impossible.
Pupil: No it isn't, teacher. I'm eight today.

Biff: I heard a new joke the other day. I wonder if I told
  it to you?
Boff: Is it funny?
Biff: Yes.
Boff: Then you didn't.

I know a lady who is so fond of arguing, she won't eat anything that agrees with her.

Customer: Waiter, I can't seem to find any oysters in this oyster soup.
Waiter: Would you expect to find angels in angel cake?

The U.S. Government reports that 30 million people are overweight. These, of course, are only round figures.

Teacher: Sammy, please give me an example of a double negative.
Sammy: I don't know none.
Teacher: Correct, thank you!

A little boy came home from his first day at school.

"I'm not going back tomorrow," he said.

"Why not, dear?" his mother asked.

"Well, I can't read and I can't write, and they won't let me talk—so what's the use?"

Baby Skunk: Can I have a chemistry set?
Mama Skunk: What! And smell up the house?

"I didn't send for a piano tuner," said the puzzled housewife.

"No," replied the piano tuner, "the people next door did."

A tourist stopped at a country gas station. While his car was being serviced, he noticed an old-timer basking in the sun with a piece of rope in his hand. The tourist walked up to the old-timer and asked, "What do you have there?"

"That's a weather gauge, sonny," the old-timer replied.

"How can you possibly tell the weather with a piece of rope?"

"It's simple," said the old-timer. "When it swings back and forth, it's windy, and when it gets wet, it's raining."

Igor: What do you have to know to teach a dog tricks?
Boris: More than the dog.

Ned: What kind of dog do you have there—a pointer?
Fred: No—a disappointer.

Flip: What do termites do when they want to relax?
Flop: They take a coffee table break.

Judge: The next man who raises his voice in the court will be thrown out.
Prisoner: Hip, hip hooray!

Ike: Do you have holes in your underwear?
Mike: How insulting! Of course I don't have holes in my underwear.
Ike: Then how do you get your feet through?

Sam: My great-grandfather fought with Napoleon, my grandfather fought with the French, and my father fought with the Americans.

Pam: Your folks couldn't get along with anybody, could they?

Igor: Did you hear the story about the man who lives on onions alone?

Boris: No. But any man who lives on onions ought to live alone.

Two explorers were going through the jungle when a ferocious lion appeared in front of them.

"Keep calm," said the first explorer. "Remember what we read in that book on wild animals? If you stand absolutely still and look the lion straight in the eye, he will turn tail and run."

"Fine," said the second explorer. "You've read the book, and I've read the book, but has the lion read the book?"

Tip: Stop acting like a fool!

Top: I'm not acting.

A cannibal mother and her child heard the sound of an airplane and looked up. The child had never seen an airplane before and asked its mother what it was.

"It's something like a can of sardines," she explained. "You open it up and eat what is inside."

Two boy scouts from the city were on a camping trip. The mosquitoes were so fierce, the boys had to hide under their blankets to avoid being bitten. One of them saw some lightning bugs and said to his friend, "We might as well give up. They're coming after us with flashlights."

Dit: Swimming is one of the best exercises for keeping the body slim and trim.
Dot: Did you ever see a whale?

Ecology is everyone's problem. A friend of mine went to the doctor for water on the knee. When the doctor made tests, it turned out the water was polluted.

Boy: Doc, my rabbit is sick. I can't understand it—I
don't feed him anything but hair tonic.

Veterinarian: Hair tonic? That's the trouble. Don't you
know you're not supposed to use that greasy kid's
stuff on your hare?

Patient: You were right, doctor, when you said you
would have me on my feet and walking around in no
time.

Doctor: I'm glad to hear you say that. When did you
start walking?

Patient: Right after I sold my car to pay your bill.

Patient: My head is stuffed, my sinuses need draining
and my chest feels like lead. Can you help me?

Doctor: You need a plumber, not a doctor.

"My brother is so strong he tore up a pack of cards with one hand."

"That's nothing. My brother rushed out the door this morning and tore up the street."

Have you heard about the new electric ruler? Turn it on and it rules the world.

Wise man says:

You can fool some of the people all of the time; and all of the people some of the time; but the rest of the time they will make fools of themselves.

Learn from the mistakes of others, because you can't live long enough to make them all by yourself.

When everything's coming your way, you're probably in the wrong lane.

Nothing is all wrong. Even a broken clock is right twice a day.

Keep your words soft and sweet—you never know when you might have to eat them.

Show me a man who always stands on his own two feet and I'll show you a man who can't get his pants on.

Even Mason and Dixon had to draw the line somewhere.

Did you hear what the termite said when he walked into the saloon? He said, "Is the bar tender here?"

Teacher: Harold, if one and one makes two, and two and two makes four, how much does four and four make?

Harold: That isn't fair, teacher. You answer the easy ones yourself, and leave the hard ones for us.

Teacher: Why are you late, Joseph?

Joseph: Because of a sign down the road.

Teacher: What does a sign have to do with your being late?

Joseph: The sign said, "School Ahead, Go Slow!"

Then there was this guy who was so dumb he thought the Red Sea was parted with a sea-saw.

Biff: Only fools are certain. Wise men hesitate.

Boff: Are you sure of that?

Biff: I'm certain.

7 Crazies

Patient: Doctor, you must help me. I can't remember anything.
Doctor: How long has this been going on?
Patient: How long has what been going on?

Customer: Waiter, are you sure this ham was cured?
Waiter: Certainly, sir.
Customer: From its taste, I would say it's still sick.

Customer: Waiter, what kind of soup is this? I ordered pea soup, this tastes like soap.
Waiter: My mistake, that's tomato soup. Pea soup tastes like gasoline.

Waiter: I have boiled tongue, fried liver, and pigs' feet.
Customer: Waiter, I'm not interested in your medical problems, just bring me a cheese sandwich and a glass of milk.

Sam: I'm having a lot of trouble with eczema, teacher.
Teacher: Heavens, where do you have it?
Sam: I don't have it, I just can't spell it.

An excited woman telephoned her doctor, "Doctor, doctor, my husband swallowed a mouse! What shall I do?

"Wave a piece of cheese in front of his mouth until I get there," the doctor said.

Fifteen minutes later he arrived at the house to find the woman waving a sardine in front of her husband's mouth.

"I said a piece of cheese, not a sardine!" exclaimed the doctor.

"I know you did," the woman replied, "But I have to get the cat out first."

Farmer: On my farm we go to bed with the chickens.
City Man: In the city, we'd rather sleep in our own beds.